THE WILD WEST TRIVIA SERIES:

OREGON TRAIL
TRIVIA

BY RICK STEBER

Copyright © 2017
by Rick Steber

All rights reserved. No part of the material protected by this copyright notice may be reproduced or utilized in any form or by any means, electronic or mechanical, including photocopying, recording or by any informational storage and retrieval system without written permission from the copyright owner.

ISBN: 978-0-945134-48-0

Printed and bound in the United States of America by
Maverick Publications • Bend, Oregon

OREGON TRAIL

THE WILD WEST TRIVIA SERIES:

Oregon Trail Trivia is one book from the Wild West Trivia series. Each book is designed to challenge a reader's knowledge and expertise relating to American history, the great outdoors and the wide panorama of the Western landscape. This series is educational and a fun way for children, friends and families to learn. Oftentimes a question or answer will serve as a springboard into other discussions, remembrances or related stories.

Turn *Oregon Trail Trivia* into an entertaining game by having one person read a question aloud. The opponent, or team of players, selects an answer.

The reader turns the page and reads aloud the correct answer. This is a wonderful way to pass the miles while traveling, or as rousing entertainment around a crackling campfire. Have fun while you learn, and keep score if you wish. Collect the entire series.

QUESTION

How many pioneers traveled over the Oregon Trail?

    A. One-quarter million
    B. One million
    C. Two million

ANSWER ON
NEXT PAGE

ANSWER

Although no record exists of exactly how many people said goodbye to family and friends and struck out over the prairie to the American West, historians believe that between 250,000 and 500,000 travelers crossed the Oregon Trail by wagon.

QUESTION

What was the first wheeled vehicle to cross the Continental Divide?

    A. Cart with a cannon
    B. Mormon cart
    C. Covered wagon

ANSWER ON NEXT PAGE

ANSWER

The first wheeled vehicle to reach the Oregon Country was a cart carrying a six-pound cannon. In 1827 fur trader William Ashley dragged this cannon to the trading fort he built on the shore of the Great Salt Lake.

QUESTION

What river, which would later provide the basis for American claim to the Oregon Country, did Captain Robert Gray lay claim to in 1792?

- A. Sacramento River
- B. Snake River
- C. Columbia River

ANSWER ON
NEXT PAGE

ANSWER

Captain Robert Gray sailed into the Columbia River on May 11, 1792. He named it the Columbia River and claimed all the land drained by this great river for the United States. This provided legal justification for the American wagon pioneers to settle in the Oregon Country.

QUESTION

What Missouri town, built around a brick courthouse, was one of the main jumping off points on the Oregon Trail?

  A. Kansas City
  B. Independence
  C. Jefferson City

ANSWER ON NEXT PAGE

ANSWER

Several routes from the Mississippi Valley converged at Independence, Missouri. This town was the last significant supply point for early emigrants headed west. Businesses clustered around a brick courthouse catered to the needs of Oregon Trail emigrants. A rail fence was built to protect the courthouse lawn from the pioneers' stock.

QUESTION

When did the first wagons reach the Rocky Mountains?

    A. 1805
    B. 1811
    C. 1830

ANSWER ON
NEXT PAGE

ANSWER

In 1830 William Sublette, David Jackson and Jedediah Smith took ten wagons, pulled by five mules each, on a route up the Platte River to the Wind River rendezvous. The wagons carried 1,800 pounds of trade goods and supplies and were able to make between 15 and 25 miles a day.

QUESTION

What epidemic swept through the Mississippi Valley in 1843?

    A. Bubonic plague
    B. Yellow fever
    C. Measles

ANSWER ON
NEXT PAGE

ANSWER

An epidemic of yellow fever swept through the Mississippi Valley in 1843, killing an estimated 13,000 people. This infectious disease, transmitted to humans by mosquitoes, caused many people to consider loading their wagons and moving west to Oregon, an area which was considered disease-free.

QUESTION

What sign was posted at the "parting-of-the-ways" on the Oregon Trail, one way leading to California and the other to Oregon?

    A. "On to Oregon"
    B. "Oregon – visit but don't stay"
    C. "Gold rush next left"

ANSWER ON NEXT PAGE

ANSWER

It was said that at the "parting-of-the-ways", where the California Trail swung south and away from the Oregon Trail, a sign was posted simply stating, "On to Oregon". It was jokingly said that those who could read came to Oregon, all the others went to California.

QUESTION

What historical event had the largest impact on the Oregon Trail?

- A. War with Great Britain
- B. Presidential election of 1844
- C. Gold rush

ANSWER ON NEXT PAGE

ANSWER

On January 23, 1848 James Marshall discovered gold nuggets along the American River in California. This discovery led to the greatest gold rush in history. Most of the men who came west hoping to strike it rich traveled over the Oregon Trail, taking one of the numerous cutoffs that led to California.

QUESTION

What was "Oregon Fever"?

- A. Desire to move west
- B. An epidemic of sickness that swept the Mississippi Valley
- C. Sickness that occurred when pioneers reached Oregon

ANSWER ON NEXT PAGE

ANSWER

Several factors caused "Oregon Fever" including a national depression, poor prices for agricultural goods, epidemics sweeping through the Mississippi Valley and the all-too-familiar predictability of life. A man struck with "Oregon Fever" was willing to trek westward for free land and the vague belief that life would be better in the far West.

QUESTION

What mountain range did wagon travelers have to cross on the California cutoff of the Oregon Trail?

    A. Cascade Mountains
    B. Blue Mountains
    C. Sierra Nevada

ANSWER ON
NEXT PAGE

ANSWER

The California cutoff led across the high desert where the trail was sandy, the temperatures were hot and water was scarce. At the far edge of this plain the pioneers were faced with a difficult climb up and over the high Sierra Nevada. They reached this point late in the fall, always with the threat of being trapped by snow in the mountains.

QUESTION

What was the number one cause of death on the Oregon Trail?

- A. Disease
- B. Indian attack
- C. Accidental gunshots

ANSWER ON
NEXT PAGE

ANSWER

It is a common misbelief that Indians killed many pioneers. The pioneers' real enemy was disease, and cholera was the worst. Cholera was spread by poor sanitation at camping areas. In almost all cases death came within a few hours. Some wagon trains lost more than half of their numbers to this dreaded disease.

QUESTION

What percentage of the pioneers died attempting to cross the Oregon Trail?

    A. 1 in 10
    B. 1 in 100
    C. 1 in 500

ANSWER ON
NEXT PAGE

ANSWER

It was said that the Oregon Trail was the longest graveyard in the history of the world. Historians believe that 1 in 10 died and were buried in graves along the trail.

QUESTION

What national event signaled the end of the Oregon Trail?

- A. Presidential election
- B. Invention of the airplane
- C. Transcontinental railroad

ANSWER ON NEXT PAGE

ANSWER

The glory years of the Oregon Trail ended with the 1869 completion of the transcontinental railroad to California. However, emigrants who could not afford passage on the railroad, or who wanted to see the country, continued to travel the Oregon Trail. Only after the advent of the automobile did wagon travel over the Oregon Trail cease to exist.

QUESTION

What was the second leading cause of death on the Oregon Trail?

- A. Indian attack
- B. Disease
- C. Accidental shooting

ANSWER ON
NEXT PAGE

ANSWER

The second leading cause of death for the pioneers was accidental shootings. Every man carried a loaded weapon for protection and hunting. The rifles could easily be discharged by jostling wagons or improper handling.

QUESTION

How did the Lewis and Clark Expedition benefit the Oregon Trail?

    A. Blazed the route
    B. Provided maps and a wealth of scientific data
    C. Established American ownership of the Oregon Country

ANSWER ON NEXT PAGE

ANSWER

Upon reaching the Pacific Ocean William Clark wrote: "We now discover that we have found the most practicable and navigable passage across the continent...." But Clark was wrong. No pioneer would follow the Expedition's difficult trail. However, the Corps did provide detailed maps and notes and a wealth of solid scientific data about the Far West.

QUESTION

Name the spot on the Oregon Trail that crosses over the backbone of the North American continent.

- A. North Pass
- B. South Pass
- C. Hidden Pass

ANSWER ON
NEXT PAGE

ANSWER

In 1812 Robert Stuart, leading a party of men from Fort Astoria to St. Louis, discovered a break in the Rocky Mountains. In later years this 20-mile-wide pathway, named South Pass, provided a passage where wagons could easily cross over the Continental Divide.

QUESTION

Name the first route traversed by wheeled vehicles across the Cascades Mountains.

- A. Applegate Trail
- B. Barlow Trail
- C. Santiam Trail

ANSWER ON
NEXT PAGE

ANSWER

The Barlow Trail was founded by Samuel K. Barlow in 1845. A toll road was established the following year and many wagon emigrants passed over this route, crossing the southern flank of Mt. Hood, on their way to the Willamette Valley.

QUESTION

About how many months did it take the early-day Oregon Trail pioneers to travel the 2,000 miles from Missouri to the Willamette Valley?

- A. Four months
- B. Six months
- C. A year

ANSWER ON NEXT PAGE

ANSWER

B

The journey from Missouri to Oregon took about six months. Pioneers departed from Missouri as early in the spring as travel was possible, usually in April or May. They arrived in Oregon between September and late November.

QUESTION

About how many miles a day did the pioneers figure a team of oxen, pulling a covered wagon, could travel?

    A. One or two miles
    B. Twelve to twenty miles
    C. Thirty to forty miles

ANSWER ON NEXT PAGE

ANSWER

B

Oxen were slow but steady beasts of burden. They traveled at a pace of about two miles per hour and in an average day could be counted on to pull a wagon between twelve and twenty miles.

QUESTION

Why did pioneers name a particular point on the Snake River "Farewell Bend"?

- A. That was where the California Trail veered away from the Oregon Trail
- B. The origin of the Applegate Trail
- C. The point where the Oregon Trail left the Snake River

ANSWER ON NEXT PAGE

ANSWER

Farewell Bend marked the point where the pioneers veered away from the Snake River, which they had followed for 330 miles, and began the difficult crossing of the Blue Mountains.

QUESTION

What is Sam Barlow known for?

   A. Trail blazing
   B. Exploring the Oregon coast
   C. Belonging to the Lewis and Clark Expedition

ANSWER ON
NEXT PAGE

ANSWER

Sam Barlow was a trail blazer who, in 1846, constructed a toll road that extended the Oregon Trail over the Cascade Mountains. He was quoted as saying: "God never made a mountain that he didn't make a way to get over it." In 1846 he established a toll road over the southern flank of Mt. Hood to the Willamette Valley.

QUESTION

What desert did the Applegate Cutoff cross?

- A. Black Rock Desert
- B. Great Salt Lake
- C. Red Rock Desert

ANSWER ON NEXT PAGE

ANSWER

The Applegate Cutoff, sometimes called the Southern Road, provided an alternate route to the Willamette Valley that bypassed both the Blue Mountains and rafting down the Columbia River. The Cutoff began at Fort Hall, crossed the torturous Black Rock Desert and wound its way across the southern Cascades into the Willamette Valley.

QUESTION

What type of wagons did the pioneers use to cross the Oregon Trail?

- A. Conestoga wagons
- B. Buckboards
- C. Farm wagons

ANSWER ON NEXT PAGE

ANSWER

Conestoga wagons were much too heavy and unwieldy to be used on the westward migration. Emigrants used farm wagons in which the undercarriage was centered around a kingpin which allowed the front wheels to pivot and the wagon to be easily turned.

QUESTION

With what did the pioneers treat the wagon covers to keep them from leaking?

    A. Spray Guard
    B. Linseed oil
    C. Axle grease

ANSWER ON NEXT PAGE

WILD WEST TRIVIA

ANSWER

B

The cloth covers, fastened to bows, protected the contents of the wagon. The ends were typically drawn shut to keep out the incessant dust. The covers were treated with linseed oil to shed the rain but eventually most of them leaked anyway.

QUESTION

How large was the wagon box on the typical Oregon Trail wagon?

- A. 4 feet by 10 feet
- B. 8 feet by 14 feet
- C. 12 feet by 20 feet

ANSWER ON NEXT PAGE

WILD WEST TRIVIA

ANSWER

The typical wagon box measured only 4 feet by 10 feet. This small space was loaded with up to a ton of cargo including food, furniture and farming implements for use when the pioneers reached their new home out west.

QUESTION

What was carried in a bucket that hung under the rear axle of every wagon that came west?

   A. Water
   B. Grease
   C. Linseed oil

ANSWER ON NEXT PAGE

ANSWER

B

The bucket that hung off the rear axle of every wagon that came west carried grease to lubricate the hubs of the wagon wheels.

QUESTION

In what year did Willamette Valley residents organize the Provisional Government of Oregon?

    A. 1812
    B. 1831
    C. 1843

ANSWER ON
NEXT PAGE

ANSWER

C

In 1843 legendary mountain man Joe Meek drew a line on the ground and said that anyone who wanted to challenge the British claim of sovereignty to the Oregon Country should step over the line. Two French-Canadians, F.X. Matthieu and Etienne Lucier, broke a deadlock for the American interests. This action allowed for legal settlement of the Willamette Valley.

QUESTION

What animal did most early-day emigrants choose to pull their wagons?

- A. Horses
- B. Mules
- C. Oxen

ANSWER ON
NEXT PAGE

ANSWER

C

Oxen were used by most pioneers. The animals were big, strong, durable and could pull a heavy load. Oxen were also less expensive than mules or horses, were not prone to running away or stampeding, and they would eat almost anything. The oxen's single drawback was being a lumbering animal capable of traveling only about 2 miles per hour.

QUESTION

What did the able-bodied women and children do while crossing the Oregon Trail?

    A. Rode in the wagon
    B. Rode horseback
    C. Walked

ANSWER ON NEXT PAGE

ANSWER

C

Rather than add their weight to the load, and take a chance of overworking the oxen, mules or horses, all the able-bodied women and children walked. Many made the entire 2,000-mile journey on foot, wearing out several pairs of shoes in the process.

QUESTION

While crossing the Plains what was the pioneers' greatest obstacle?

    A. Lack of food
    B. Indian attacks
    C. Weather

ANSWER ON NEXT PAGE

ANSWER

C

While crossing the Plains fierce lightning storms struck the wagon trains and at times they were pelted by giant hail, buffeted by wild wind storms, rain and even tornadoes. Oregon trail emigrants were at the mercy of the weather and when a bad storm struck there was no place for them to hide.

QUESTION

Why did the pioneers circle their wagons at night?

    A. It looked good in photographs
    B. To corral the livestock
    C. Protection against Indians

ANSWER ON
NEXT PAGE

ANSWER

B

Even though Hollywood movies have fueled the myth that pioneers circled the wagons at the end of the day as protection against Indian attacks, the circled wagons provided a convenient corral for loose livestock.

QUESTION

What did the pioneers use for campfire fuel when wood was scarce?

- A. Buffalo chips
- B. Propane stoves
- C. Wood they brought along

ANSWER ON NEXT PAGE

ANSWER

Trees were scarce on the Plains but the pioneers found plenty of dry buffalo chips to fuel their fires. The women would collect the buffalo chips, usually carrying them in their aprons. About 3½ bushels of buffalo chips were required for an evening's campfire.

QUESTION

From what state did most of the Oregon Trail pioneers originate?

    A. Missouri
    B. Kansas
    C. Ohio

ANSWER ON NEXT PAGE

ANSWER

Most of the Oregon Trail pioneers were residents of Missouri. One historian claimed that more than half the emigrants who died on the Trail were Missourians. According to the 1850 census, one-quarter of all Oregon residents listed Missouri as their home state.

OREGON TRAIL

QUESTION

Why was the railroad rerouted a few feet near Scottsbluff, Nebraska?

    A. Preserve Oregon Trail ruts
    B. Preserve a grave
    C. Preserve an Oregon Trail marker

ANSWER ON NEXT PAGE

ANSWER

B

The railroad, built in 1902, was rerouted to avoid the grave of Rebecca Winters who died of cholera in August 1852. The remains were moved 900 feet in 1995 and a memorial was established for Rebecca along the East Beltline highway between the towns of Gering and Scottsbluff, Nebraska.

QUESTION

How long did it take passengers from the east coast to reach the Pacific Northwest by ship?

- A. One month
- B. Six months
- C. Eight months

ANSWER ON NEXT PAGE

ANSWER

For travelers who did not care to face the hardships of the Oregon Trail, the only alternative to reach the west coast was passage on a ship. Such a journey was very expensive and took a minimum of eight months to sail around the horn of South America and up the coast to California or the Pacific Northwest.

QUESTION

What was the record for the number of people passing through Fort Laramie in a single day?

- A. 1,000 people
- B. 3,000 people
- C. 6,000 people

ANSWER ON NEXT PAGE

ANSWER

The single-day record for people passing through Fort Laramie occurred on June 17, 1850. Most of the 6,034 travelers were headed to California to seek their fortunes in the gold fields.

QUESTION

What did pioneer women and girls wear to protect themselves from the sun?

- A. Sun block
- B. Sunglasses
- C. Bonnets

ANSWER ON
NEXT PAGE

ANSWER

C

In order to protect their complexion and hair from the harsh sun and the constant wind, many of the women and girls who crossed the Oregon Trail chose to wear sunbonnets.

QUESTION

About how much did it cost a family to travel over the Oregon Train in the 1850s?

   A. $500
   B. $1,000
   C. $3,000

ANSWER ON
NEXT PAGE

ANSWER

In addition to a wagon and oxen, which cost about $300, pioneers were urged to take plenty of food, pots, pans and utensils, water pails, candles, matches, hand tools and farming equipment. The minimum cost for a family moving west in the 1850s was about $500.

QUESTION

Why did Jesse and Lindsay Applegate vow to search for a safer wagon route to the Willamette Valley?

    A. To profit from establishing a toll road
    B. Because of a drowning
    C. For political gain

ANSWER ON NEXT PAGE

ANSWER

B

The Applegate family came west over the Oregon Trail in 1843. As they rafted through the rapids on the Columbia River, Lindsay's son Warren and Jesse's son Edward, both 9 years old, drowned. This terrible tragedy made the brothers determined to find a safer route. In 1846 they opened the Applegate Cutoff that veered away from the Oregon Trail at Fort Hall.

QUESTION

In what year did the first white women cross the Rocky Mountains?

    A. 1806
    B. 1836
    C. 1843

ANSWER ON NEXT PAGE

ANSWER

B

In 1836 Narcissa Whitman and Eliza Spaulding accompanied their husbands to the Oregon Country, becoming the first white women to cross the Rocky Mountains. They traveled by wagon as far as Fort Boise where the wagons were abandoned.

QUESTION

What happened to the original Fort Bridger?

- A. Sold
- B. Burned
- C. Abandoned

ANSWER ON
NEXT PAGE

ANSWER

Mountain man Jim Bridger established Fort Bridger in the early 1840s. He sold goods and supplies to Oregon Trail emigrants but the business tied him down and apparently Bridger abandoned his outpost. One hundred years later the site of Bridger's original fort, located near Fort Bridger, Wyoming, was destroyed to obtain rock for road maintenance.

QUESTION

What strange contraption did Rufus Porter propose in 1849 to ferry passengers to the west coast?

    A. Bullet train
    B. Airline
    C. Automobile

ANSWER ON NEXT PAGE

ANSWER

B

Inventor Rufus Porter developed a grand scheme to build a fleet of balloons with propellers powered by steam engines to ferry passengers to the West. He advertised his airline and received 200 reservations but none of his airships ever got off the ground.

QUESTION

What is the most intriguing part of the story of the "Lone Grave"?

    A. The death of the person buried there
    B. Location of the grave
    C. The grave marker

ANSWER ON NEXT PAGE

ANSWER

C

Pioneer Susan Hail died from cholera on June 2, 1852. Her husband returned to the settlement of St. Joe for a tombstone. After the marble was inscribed he loaded it in a wheelbarrow which he pushed 300 miles to mark his wife's grave. Today a monument near Kenesaw, Nebraska is dedicated to the final resting spot of Susan Hail.

QUESTION

What was the first military fort built along the route of the Oregon Trail?

- A. Fort Bridger
- B. Fort Platte
- C. Fort Kearney

ANSWER ON
NEXT PAGE

ANSWER

C

Fort Kearney, located along the Platte River 300 miles west of Independence, was the first military post built to protect Oregon Trail emigrants. It was composed of sod and adobe buildings. Pioneers often stopped here to purchase food and necessities. Fort Kearney remained an important wayside along the trail until the 1870s.

QUESTION

What other means of travel did Ezra Meeker, pioneer of 1852, employ to travel the Oregon Trail?

    A. Wheel cart
    B. Airplane
    C. Bus

ANSWER ON NEXT PAGE

ANSWER

B

Ezra Meeker, who some consider the Father of the Oregon Trail for his efforts to mark and preserve the Trail, came west by ox team in 1852. In 1907, at the age of 75, he recreated that trip in a wagon traveling east and met with President Teddy Roosevelt. He also traveled the route in an automobile and in 1924, at the age of 93, he flew over the trail in an airplane.

QUESTION

What was the first steep grade encountered by travelers on the Oregon Trail?

- A. Windlass Hill
- B. Laurel Hill
- C. Blue Mountains

ANSWER ON NEXT PAGE

ANSWER

Windlass Hill, located 500 miles west of Independence, dropped into the ravine at Ash Hollow. The Trail descended 150 feet in the distance of a football field and many pioneers were compelled to let their wagons down by rope rather than run the risk of killing their stock or overturning their wagons.

QUESTION

What is the name of the sandstone feature which stands near Courthouse Rock?

- A. Jail Rock
- B. Chimney Rock
- C. Independence Rock

ANSWER ON
NEXT PAGE

ANSWER

Courthouse Rock, and the smaller Jail Rock which stands nearby, are located 560 miles west of Independence. They were the first impressive geological features the pioneers encountered and diaries tell of side trips taken by people who took time to climb and carve their names into these sandstone features.

QUESTION

What landmark is most often noted in the diaries of the pioneers?

   A. Scotts Bluff
   B. Columbia River
   C. Chimney Rock

ANSWER ON NEXT PAGE

ANSWER

C

Chimney Rock, located 575 miles from Independence, is a prominent column of clay and sandstone that resembles a tall chimney. From the broad base to the tip, the column is over 300 feet. This landmark is mentioned in nearly every pioneer diary because the sight of it was so unique and memorable.

QUESTION

How deep were ruts carved into the sandstone at Mitchell Pass?

- A. Two feet
- B. Eight feet
- C. Twenty feet

ANSWER ON
NEXT PAGE

ANSWER

B

In order to avoid the massive sandstone formation at Scotts Bluff, 596 miles west of Independence, Missouri, emigrants took the narrow route through Mitchell Pass. Today the ruts, located near the town of Gering, Nebraska, are eight feet deep and stand as mute testimony to the number of wagons that passed this way.

QUESTION

What led to the massacre of Lt. John Grattan and his 29 men at the hands of Sioux Indians near Fort Laramie, Wyoming?

- A. War had been declared
- B. A cow
- C. A rifle accidentally discharged

ANSWER ON NEXT PAGE

ANSWER

B

On August 19, 1854 a cow wandered away from a group of Mormon emigrants and into the nearby camp of Sioux Indians who promptly killed and ate the stray. Lt. John Grattan and his 29 men attempted to arrest the chief of the Sioux, The Bear, for stealing the cow. When the chief was killed the Indians killed all the soldiers.

QUESTION

What fort marked the gateway to the Rocky Mountains?

  A. Fort McPherson
  B. Fort Bridger
  C. Fort Laramie

ANSWER ON
NEXT PAGE

ANSWER

C

Fort Laramie was a welcome sight for the pioneers. It was mid-point of their journey and heralded the approach of the Continental Divide. William Sublette built a fur trading post at this location in 1834. The U.S. government purchased Fort Laramie to serve as an army post to protect the emigrants from the Sioux Indians.

QUESTION

Who was Mary Homsley?

- A. First woman to cross the Blue Mountains
- B. Woman who died on the Oregon Trail crossing
- C. Wife of mountain man Jim Bridger

ANSWER ON NEXT PAGE

ANSWER

B

In 1934 a stone inscribed "Grave of Mary E. Homsley, died June 10, 1852" was found near Fort Laramie. A news article asked the question, "Who was Mary Homsley?" Mrs. Laura Gibson of Portland, Oregon responded that 73 years earlier, at the age of three, she had witnessed her mother's burial but never knew the location of the grave until reading the newspaper story.

QUESTION

What caused the loss of many pioneer names carved into Register Cliff?

    A. Vandals
    B. Earthquake
    C. Natural erosion

ANSWER ON
NEXT PAGE

ANSWER

Register Cliff, located near Guernsey, Wyoming, is a mile-long sandstone rock where many pioneers carved their names and dates of passing. Unfortunately, in recent times, the cliff face has been vandalized by people chipping off souvenirs or defacing the earlier writings. Today a chain-link fence protects a portion of the writing from vandals.

QUESTION

Where was the Mormon Ferry located?

- A. There was no such ferry
- B. North Platte River
- C. Green River

ANSWER ON
NEXT PAGE

ANSWER

B

The Mormon Ferry was established by Mormons in 1847 at the crossing of the North Platte River, near present-day Casper, Wyoming. The fee charged, from four to five dollars per wagon, helped the Mormons finance their growing settlement at Great Salt Lake. The ferry was abandoned when a bridge was built in 1851.

QUESTION

From a distance what does Independence Rock resemble?

- A. Turtle
- B. Flag
- C. Fireworks

ANSWER ON NEXT PAGE

ANSWER

Independence Rock, located along the Oregon Trail 814 miles west of Independence, is a giant outcropping of granite which, from a distance, resembles the shell of a giant turtle. Pioneers tried to reach this point by the 4th of July.

QUESTION

Which river created Devil's Gate, an important landmark on the Oregon Trail?

- A. North Platte River
- B. Snake River
- C. Sweetwater River

ANSWER ON NEXT PAGE

ANSWER

C

Devil's Gate is a narrow gorge carved by the Sweetwater River. In the early 1860s four young women from a wagon train climbed the ridge above the gorge. One of the young ladies fell and her grave board was inscribed: "Here lies the body of Caroline Todd, Whose soul had lately gone to God; Ere redemption was too late, She was redeemed at Devil's Gate."

QUESTION

What was the most important landmark on the Oregon Trail?

    A. Independence Rock
    B. South Pass
    C. Columbia River

ANSWER ON
NEXT PAGE

ANSWER

B

Without South Pass, the low-elevation crossing of the Rocky Mountains, wagon travel across the continent would have been nearly impossible. The approach from the east is an imperceptible grade into the pass that is 20-miles wide. Most pioneers did not realize they had crossed the backbone of the continent until noticing streams running toward the Pacific Ocean.

QUESTION

What was unusual about the proprietor of Smith's Trading Post, located near the present town of Montpelier, Idaho?

- A. He had a wooden leg and dressed like a sea captain
- B. He was a religious man who quoted scripture
- C. He wrestled a tame bear for money

ANSWER ON NEXT PAGE

ANSWER

Peg Leg Smith established a trading post on Bear River, below the outlet of Bear Lake. It was reported that the former mountain man had injured his leg, amputated it himself with his hunting knife and carved its replacement from a hunk of wood. Emigrants noted that Peg Leg Smith liked to dress in navy blue and white, like a steamboat captain in St. Louis.

QUESTION

There are two springs at milepost 1154 on the Oregon Trail in present Bear Valley, Idaho. One is named Soda Springs. What is the other spring named?

    A. Beer
    B. Geyser
    C. Cola

ANSWER ON NEXT PAGE

ANSWER

Rufus Sage noted in his journal in 1842 that the Bear Valley springs emitted a hissing noise and that "...the water of the one tastes to be excellent natural soda, and the other, slightly acid and beer like.... These natural curiosities are known among the trappers as Soda and Beer springs, names not altogether inappropriate."

QUESTION

At what western fort were pioneers encouraged to either turn around and return east or head south to California?

- A. Fort Vancouver
- B. Fort Hall
- C. Fort Bridger

ANSWER ON
NEXT PAGE

ANSWER

B

When Fort Hall was completed by Nathaniel Wyeth it was the only outpost owned by an American in the entire Oregon Country. In 1837 he sold the fort to the Hudson's Bay Company and the British flag flew over Fort Hall. The British at the fort discouraged travel to Oregon, saying homesteading was forbidden and that Britain controlled all the land to the west.

QUESTION

What geological feature amazed pioneers who chose to take the Goodale Cutoff across present southern Idaho?

    A. Remains of a prehistoric lake
    B. A string of geysers
    C. Lava flows

ANSWER ON NEXT PAGE

ANSWER

Beginning in the 1860s many pioneers chose to take the Goodale Cutoff, a new route that bypassed the established trail along the Snake River. The Goodale Cutoff skirted the edge of a huge lava field that covered 618 square miles. In 1924 this area was established as the Craters of the Moon National Monument.

QUESTION

American Falls, a 50-foot drop of the Snake River, was mentioned in many of the pioneers' diaries. What happened to the pioneer graves that were located near the falls?

    A. They were preserved
    B. They were moved
    C. They were drowned

ANSWER ON NEXT PAGE

ANSWER

C

In 1932 Jennie Broughton Brown wrote: "When American Falls dam was built the Reclamation Service advised against removal of the bones of the five or six pioneers buried in the fenced plot below the dam. And so now they lie beneath the waters of the lake."

QUESTION

Why was the natural feature in southern Idaho called "Massacre Rocks"?

    A. The name was coined as a tourist attraction
    B. Indian attack on pioneers
    C. Army attack on a village of Indians

ANSWER ON NEXT PAGE

ANSWER

Although several wagon trains were attacked by Indians and innocent people were killed near this site, none of the early journals call this narrowing of the Oregon Trail by the name "Massacre Rock". Evidence indicates that the name was coined by American Falls businessmen in 1927 to promote tourism in the area.

QUESTION

What can be found behind a sturdy chain-link fence along the Oregon Trail twelve miles southwest of American Falls, Idaho?

    A. Indian petroglyphs
    B. Meteorite
    C. Pioneer carvings

ANSWER ON NEXT PAGE

ANSWER

C

Register Rock is a half-buried boulder that holds many names of pioneers and the dates they passed this way. It is secured from public access behind a chain-link fence and protected from weathering by a roof. This site is now part of Idaho's Massacre Rocks State Park.

QUESTION

What major interstate highway follows the general route of the Oregon Trail through Oregon and Idaho?

   A. Interstate 84
   B. Interstate 90
   C. Interstate 70

ANSWER ON NEXT PAGE

ANSWER

Interstate 84 parallels the Columbia River before crossing the Blue Mountains. Entering Idaho the freeway follows the Snake River to American Falls. This is the general route of the Oregon Trail and there are numerous places where the modern highway is built over the top of the old wagon road.

QUESTION

As pioneers descended the Blue Mountains where was the nearest settlement where they could find a medical doctor or purchase supplies?

    A. Whitman Mission
    B. The Dalles
    C. Portland

ANSWER ON NEXT PAGE

ANSWER

Dr. Marcus and Narcissa Whitman established a Presbyterian mission eight miles west of present Walla Walla, Washington. A cutoff was found that bypassed the mission but pioneers in need of medical attention or supplies detoured to the mission until the Whitmans were massacred by Indians on November 29, 1847.

QUESTION

Near what present town did most of the Oregon Trail pioneers get their first view of the mighty Columbia River?

- A. Biggs Junction, Oregon
- B. Pendleton, Oregon
- C. Boardman, Oregon

ANSWER ON
NEXT PAGE

ANSWER

From a ridge beside Spanish Hollow, near the present town of Biggs Junction and 1,800 miles from Independence, the pioneers got their first view of the Columbia River. Within the next day or two they would have to make the decision whether to cross the Cascade Mountains on Barlow Trail or trust their fate to rafting down the treacherous Columbia River.

QUESTION

What was the last major rapid on the Columbia for those ferrying their wagons down river?

    A. Cascades
    B. The Dalles
    C. Celilo Falls

ANSWER ON
NEXT PAGE

ANSWER

Cascades, located near present Cascade Locks, Oregon was the last dangerous rapids that the pioneers faced. This section of river was almost unnavigable and required a three-mile portage around the rapids.

QUESTION

Along the Barlow Trail is a glacial boulder with the inscription, "Baby Morgan Grave". How did the baby die?

- A. Illness
- B. Accident
- C. Murdered

ANSWER ON NEXT PAGE

ANSWER

B

The death of the pioneer child shows how quickly a life could be taken on the Oregon Trail. The child was born near Independence Rock to Daniel and Rachel Morgan. On October 24, 1847, while camped at Summit Meadow on the south flank of Mt. Hood, the infant's bed was placed in the shade behind the wagon. Apparently the tailgate fell and killed the baby.

QUESTION

What was considered the toughest grade on the Oregon Trail?

    A. Windlass Hill
    B. Ladd Canyon
    C. Laurel Hill

ANSWER ON NEXT PAGE

ANSWER

Laurel Hill on the Barlow Trail was described by Walter Meacham, pioneer of 1847: "Laurel Hill is the toughest section of the Old Oregon Trail. It is a long, high, broken ridge... the oxen could not hold back the wagons... some took their wagons apart and slid them down, others cut trees and dragged them behind, others tied long ropes around trees and let their wagons down inch by inch."

QUESTION

Before gold was discovered in California, where was the largest trading center in the West located?

- A. Fort Vancouver
- B. Fort Astoria
- C. Fort Hall

ANSWER ON NEXT PAGE

ANSWER

Fort Vancouver, owned by the Hudson's Bay Company, was the largest trading center in the West. Dr. John McLaughlin, Chief Factor, provided Oregon Trail pioneers with food, lodging and transportation. He extended them credit until they could claim land and raise a crop. Because of his efforts Dr. McLaughlin was given the honorary title, "Father of Oregon".

QUESTION

When the pioneers reached the end of the Barlow Trail, considered by some to be the true end of the Oregon Trail, what did they find?

    A. Empty field
    B. Indian camp
    C. Thriving town

ANSWER ON NEXT PAGE

ANSWER

Oregon City, the terminus of the Oregon Trail, was founded by Dr. John McLoughlin in 1842. Emigrant Overton Johnson wrote: "We were happy, after a long and tedious tour, to witness the home of civilization. To see mills, storehouses, shops. To hear the noise of the workman's hammer; to enjoy the warm welcome of countrymen and friends."

QUESTION

What braking system was employed to slow and stop the pioneer wagons?

   A. Disc brakes
   B. Brake blocks
   C. Anchors tied to the wagon

ANSWER ON NEXT PAGE

ANSWER

B

The rear wheels of the wagons were outfitted with brake blocks. When the driver threw a lever it engaged the brake blocks, which were usually made from a hard wood such as oak. The brake block slowed the wagon by applying friction against the wheel.

QUESTION

Why did the prairie schooners have larger wheels on the back and smaller wheels on the front?

- A. So they would always go downhill
- B. Less drag for the animals to pull
- C. Easier turning

ANSWER ON
NEXT PAGE

ANSWER

C

The rear wheels of the prairie schooner were typically fifty inches in diameter and the front wheels were about six inches shorter. The smaller front wheels allowed the wagon to make sharper turns.

QUESTION

How were the bows for the covered wagons made?

   A. Iron rims were bent into shape
   B. Wood was soaked or steamed
   C. Fiberglass was cut

ANSWER ON
NEXT PAGE

ANSWER

B

The bows were made from strips of hardwood and soaked or steamed until the wood became pliable. Then the wood was bent into a U-shape and allowed to dry. When the cloth or canvas was stretched over the bows it made a tight cover that provided protection against the weather.

QUESTION

Where is the oldest marked grave on the Oregon Trail?

- A. Guernsey, Wyoming
- B. Along the Platte River
- C. Near Fort Kearney

ANSWER ON NEXT PAGE

ANSWER

The oldest marked grave on the Oregon Trail is that of Joel Hembree, a six-year-old boy who was killed July 18, 1843 near present Guernsey, Wyoming. Young Joel was climbing out of the moving wagon; it hit a bump, the boy fell under a wheel and the heavy wagon ran over him. In later years many other children died falling under the wagon wheels.

QUESTION

How many names were carved on Independence Rock?

- A. 5,000
- B. 20,000
- C. 50,000

ANSWER ON NEXT PAGE

ANSWER

C

Many of the pioneers who passed Independence Rock felt compelled to carve their names into the stone. In 1860 it was estimated that there were 50,000 names on the rock. One of the entrepreneurial ventures of the Mormons was to have men inscribe pioneers' names on the rock at a cost of five dollars per name.

QUESTION

What amazing discovery did the pioneers make in the shallow basin at the 6,000-foot level just below South Pass?

- A. Gold
- B. Ice
- C. Mastodon fossil

ANSWER ON NEXT PAGE

ANSWER

B

The shallow basin below South Pass was called Ice Slough. Here, beneath a covering of grass and thick tundra-like turf, could be found a layer of ice even during the hot summer months. Pioneer George Belshaw wrote on July 4, 1853: "We dug down 12 inches and found chinks of ice...and made some lemonade. It relished first rate."

QUESTION

Why were most rivers in present Wyoming so dangerous for the pioneers to cross?

- A. Few ferries
- B. The oxen were worn down
- C. The rivers were usually running high

ANSWER ON NEXT PAGE

ANSWER

The pioneers arrived in present Wyoming during July and August. This was during the time of the year when snow melts in the mountains fed streams and rivers. Crossing a flooding river over a gravel bar or in a crude ferry was always a dangerous undertaking and many pioneers lost their lives during river crossings.

QUESTION

When the Oregon Trail crossed broad flats how did the pioneers travel?

    A. The wagons remained in single file
    B. The wagons spread out across the flat
    C. When they reached flat ground they always set camp

ANSWER ON NEXT PAGE

ANSWER

B

As the wagon train traveled west the wagon wheels stirred up alkali and dust. Many pioneers tied bandanas over their noses and mouths so they could breath. When they came to a flat area the wagons spread out across the flat, traveling side-by-side, in order to avoid each other's dust.

QUESTION

How many miles did Sublette's Cutoff save from the regular route of the Oregon Trail?

- A. 46 miles
- B. 142 miles
- C. 211 miles

ANSWER ON NEXT PAGE

ANSWER

Sublette's Cutoff bypassed Fort Bridger and saved the pioneers 46 miles, or about 3 long days of travel. This popular route was arguably one of the worst sections of the Trail, crossing desolate, hostile and arid country. Some pioneers traveled this section at night rather than risk their stock's dying of thirst during the heat of the day.

QUESTION

How many miles of the route of the Oregon Trail remain free from development?

- A. 200 miles
- B. 500 miles
- C. 1000 miles

ANSWER ON NEXT PAGE

ANSWER

It is estimated that 90% of the 2,000-mile long Oregon Trail has been plowed under or paved over. Civilization has encroached on the trail with roads, pipe lines, power lines, homes and farms. When the last 200 miles of Oregon Trail ruts are gone, they will be lost forever.

QUESTION

Who was the first to use oxen on the Oregon Trail?

    A. Captain Benjamin Bonneville
    B. Jedediah Smith
    C. Dr. Marcus Whitman

ANSWER ON NEXT PAGE

ANSWER

In 1832 Captain Benjamin Bonneville brought twenty ox-drawn wagons over South Pass to Green River. These were the first oxen to be used on the Oregon Trail.

QUESTION

Who was the first man to bring a wagon to the Willamette Valley?

    A. Dr. Marcus Whitman
    B. William Ashley
    C. "Doc" Newell

ANSWER ON NEXT PAGE

ANSWER

C

In 1840 "Doc" Newell, a mountain man who had guided a missionary party as far as Fort Hall, took two wagons in payment for his services. He managed to cross the Blue Mountains and was able to bring one of the wagons down the Columbia River to the Willamette Valley. This wagon was the first to make the entire overland journey.

QUESTION

At what point along the Columbia River did the Oregon Trail end?

    A. Whitman Mission
    B. The Dalles
    C. Biggs Junction

ANSWER ON NEXT PAGE

ANSWER

B

In 1838 a Methodist mission was established at The Dalles, Oregon. Here the Oregon Trail came to a stop, blocked by the Cascade Mountains. The only way around this obstacle was to take Barlow Trail around the south flank of Mt. Hood or to ferry down the Columbia River. Either choice was fraught with dangers.

QUESTION

In what year did the first wagon train reach Oregon?

    A. 1818
    B. 1833
    C. 1843

ANSWER ON NEXT PAGE

ANSWER

The "Great Migration" of 1843 included at least 120 wagons and 875 people as well as 1,000 head of livestock. They were guided by Dr. Marcus Whitman who convinced them that wagons could be taken as far as the Cascade Mountains and then ferried down the Columbia River. That fall 700 people and a depleted herd of livestock arrived at The Dalles.

QUESTION

What was important about the Raft River Crossing?

    A. It was a difficult crossing
    B. It was the site of a major "parting of the ways"
    C. The Mormons operated a ferry here

ANSWER ON NEXT PAGE

ANSWER

B

Raft River was a major "parting of the ways" where the California Trail veered away from the Oregon Trail. It was at this point that pioneers had to make the important decision of whether to continue west for Oregon or south to California. This was also where the Applegate Trail turned away from the established trail.

QUESTION

What Snake River falls did one of the pioneers compare to Niagara Falls?

    A. Shoshone Falls
    B. Caldron Linn
    C. American Falls

ANSWER ON NEXT PAGE

ANSWER

The waters of Shoshone Falls, located along the Oregon Trail four miles northeast of present Twin Falls, Idaho, pours over a 212-foot basalt cliff. Pioneer Osborne Cross wrote on August 15, 1849 that he was surprised to hear the falls from ten miles away and "... this cascade is not surpassed by Niagara Falls."

QUESTION

What natural phenomenon surprised the pioneers near present Hagerman, Idaho?

   A. Volcanic crater
   B. Springs
   C. A geyser

ANSWER ON NEXT PAGE

ANSWER

B

After crossing miles of sand and sagebrush the pioneers were pleasantly surprised to find a series of springs gushing from the rimrock along the Snake River. They bestowed the name "Thousand Springs" on this natural phenomenon. Today the springs are not nearly as impressive because most of the water has been diverted for electricity and irrigation.

QUESTION

What choice were the pioneers forced to make at Three Island Crossing?

- A. Whether to turn south to California
- B. Whether to take the Applegate Trail
- C. Whether to cross the Snake River

ANSWER ON NEXT PAGE

ANSWER

At Three Island Crossing pioneers faced the difficult choice of staying on the south side of the Snake River and following it as it swung in a big bend, or to cross the river and take a more direct route to Fort Boise. Generally half of the emigrants would choose the shortcut and use the islands in the Snake River as "stepping stones" across the treacherous current.

QUESTION

What American post was established 500 miles from the Willamette Valley to protect the emigrants as they passed along the Snake River?

    A. Fort Boise
    B. Fort Hall
    C. Fort Walla Walla

ANSWER ON NEXT PAGE

ANSWER

Fort Boise was originally built by the British Hudson's Bay Company but the location was plagued by Snake River flooding. The fort was abandoned and in 1863 a new Fort Boise was established by Oregon and Washington volunteers 50 miles to the east to protect traffic on the Oregon Trail and miners flocking to the gold mines of Idaho.

QUESTION

What Baker Valley, Oregon landmark did vandals destroy in 1843?

    A. A prominent spire
    B. A pine tree
    C. An Indian burial ground

ANSWER ON NEXT PAGE

ANSWER

B

On the floor of Baker Valley, below the foot of Flagstaff Hill, stood a towering lone pine tree that served as a prominent landmark to travelers. In September 1843 pioneer Peter Burnett wrote: "This noble tree stood in the center of a most lovely valley...but the tree has been fallen by the vandals hands... Some of our inconsiderate people cut it down for fuel."

QUESTION

What Oregon valley was known as the "Great Circle"?

    A. Baker Valley
    B. Grande Ronde Valley
    C. Powder River Valley

ANSWER ON NEXT PAGE

ANSWER

B

Pioneers found the Grande Ronde Valley, located along the edge of the Blue Mountains, to be a paradise. In 1843 explorer John C. Fremont described the valley in his journal: "The Grand Rond is a beautiful level basin, or mountain valley, covered with good grass, on a rich soil, abundantly watered...its name descriptive of its form—the great circle."

QUESTION

Which town along the Oregon Trail became the official capital of the United States for a day?

- A. Boise, Idaho
- B. Cheyenne, Wyoming
- C. Meacham, Oregon

ANSWER ON NEXT PAGE

ANSWER

On July 3, 1923 President Warren G. Harding visited the town of Meacham, Oregon, located at the summit of the Blue Mountains. He paid tribute to the old Oregon Trail and opened a new era by dedicating the Oregon Trail Highway. He officially proclaimed Meacham as the capital of the United States for that day.

QUESTION

What was the first chain of timbered mountains the pioneers encountered on their trip west?

- A. Bitterroot Range
- B. Blue Mountains
- C. Cascade Range

ANSWER ON NEXT PAGE

ANSWER

B

Most of the pioneers had lived their lives on the flat lands of the Mississippi Valley. When they reached the Blue Mountains of Oregon they were fearful of the steep grades and the narrow trail that wound through the deep forest to the 4,100-foot summit of the pass.

QUESTION

What was the halfway point on the Oregon Trail?

    A. Independence Rock
    B. South Pass
    C. Green River

ANSWER ON
NEXT PAGE

ANSWER

B

South Pass marked the midpoint of the Oregon Trail and the beginning of the Oregon Country, which stretched from the summit of the Rocky Mountains to the Pacific Ocean. When the pioneers reached this point there was little celebration because a thousand miles remained to their final destination.

WILD WEST TRIVIA

Wild West Trivia series was written and designed by award-winning author, Rick Steber. He has written more than forty books and has sold more than a million copies. For a complete listing of his books, or to see other titles in the Wild West Trivia series, visit www.ricksteber.com